I SPOT SHAPES!

I SPOT STARS

first concepts

BY NATALIE HUMPHREY

Gareth Stevens
PUBLISHING

Stars are everywhere!
The candy is a star.

3

The animal is a star.

The balloon is a star.

7

The fruit is a star.

9

The flower is a star.

11

The light is a star.

13

The toy is a star.

The cookie is a star.

The sprinkle is a star.

The badge is a star.

21

Can you spot the star?

23

Please visit our website, www.garethstevens.com. For a free color catalog of all our high-quality books, call toll free 1-800-542-2595 or fax 1-877-542-2596.

Library of Congress Cataloging-in-Publication Data
Names: Humphrey, Natalie, author.
Title: I spot stars / Natalie Humphrey.
Description: Buffalo, New York : Gareth Stevens Publishing, [2025] |
Series: I spot shapes | Includes index.
Identifiers: LCCN 2023044268 (print) | LCCN 2023044269 (ebook) | ISBN
9781538291801 (library binding) | ISBN 9781538291795 (paperback) | ISBN
9781538291818 (ebook)
Subjects: LCSH: Star (Shape)–Juvenile literature. | Shapes–Juvenile
literature. | Form perception–Juvenile literature.
Classification: LCC QA482 .H8628 2025 (print) | LCC QA482 (ebook) | DDC
516/.154–dc23/eng/20231031
LC record available at https://lccn.loc.gov/2023044268
LC ebook record available at https://lccn.loc.gov/2023044269

Published in 2025 by
Gareth Stevens Publishing
2544 Clinton Street
West Seneca, NY 14224

Designer: Leslie Taylor
Editor: Natalie Humphrey

Photo credits: Cover Belight/Shutterstock.com; p. 3 Lazhko Svetlana/Shutterstock.com; p. 5 Gary Mc Alea Photography/Shutterstock.com; p. 7 Chiociolla/Shutterstock.com; p. 9 zcw/Shutterstock.com; p. 11 Kwanbenz/Shutterstock.com; p. 13 Tanhauzer/Shutterstock.com; p. 15 All for you friend/Shutterstock.com; p. 17 r.classen/Shutterstock.com; p. 19 All For You/Shutterstock.com; p. 21 (badge) Victor Moussa/Shutterstock.com, (denim) WeerasakWooth/Shutterstock.com; p. 23 Edy Kasim/Shutterstock.com.

Printed in the United States of America

CPSIA compliance information: Batch #CSGS25: For further information contact Gareth Stevens, New York, New York at 1-800-542-2595.

Find us on